ADVANCE PRAISE (Alphabetical Order)

"Simply brilliant. Here's what I love about this book: aside from the abundance of tips, advice, and insight, the positive encouragement drips off every page. As a job seeker, I would read this book just for the encouragement, but for sure I'd learn something from every page!"

Jason Alba, CEO of JibberJobber.com and Author of 'I'm on LinkedIn—Now What??? (Second Edition)'

"Billie Sucher is one of the wisest career coaches I know. In this fabulous book, she offers over eight hundred pearls of wisdom, all served up in bite-sized pieces. From tips on resume writing to job search to interviewing, it's all covered. Listen to Billie—she knows what she's talking about!"

Louise Fletcher, President of Blue Sky Resumes, Managing Editor of Career Hub, and Author of 'The Complete Guide to Resume Writing'

"This little book provides 'twittillating' tidbits of wisdom, humor, and reflection in a very 'now' format. It stays in the crisp writing style that is definitely Billie. Don't think for a moment that one- or two-liners don't have value. Read one twittillation and you'll want another and another. Buy it, read it, keep it, and add to it!"

Steve Gallison, Gallison Associates Outplacement and Training Services

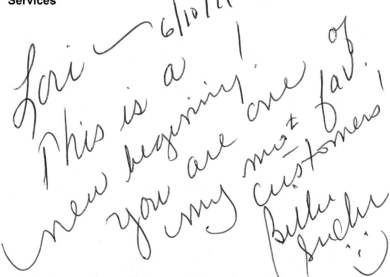

"With hundreds of valuable career books, guides, and resources available to today's job seekers, it would seem that a career expert would have to work some sort of magic for his or her book to stand out from the rest and take career advice to the next level. I am proud and excited to say that Billie Sucher has done just that. Billie has taken her exhaustive wealth of career search expertise and insight and has repackaged it into convenient, actionable, and easily-consumable tips. By harnessing the power of Twitter in her book's architecture, she has created a truly unique and engaging offering. To the job seeker who has a lot of research to do to stay on top of the search and too little time to do it in, I fully recommend you check out this book."

Chris Perry, Founder of CareerRocketeer.com

"Amongst the plethora of job search books on the market, this little book is a breath of fresh air. It's simple, yet totally on the money—timeless yet cutting edge, fun yet oh-so-very serious. If you're a job searcher looking for some quality advice in bite-sized tweets, you owe it to yourself to read this book."

Sital Ruparelia, Career and Talent Management Expert, England, UK

Happy About the Career Alphabet

An A–Z Primer for
Job Seekers of All Ages
800+ Fast & Easy Tweet-Style Tips

By Billie Sucher,
MS, CTMS, CTSB, JCTC, CCM

Foreword by Joyce Lain Kennedy

20660 Stevens Creek Blvd., Suite 210
Cupertino, CA 95014

Copyright © 2010 by Billie Sucher

First Printing: March 2010
Paperback ISBN: 1-60005-179-0 (978-1-60005-179-1)
Place of Publication: Silicon Valley, California, USA
Paperback Library of Congress Number: 2010924570
eBook ISBN: 1-60005-180-4 (978-1-60005-180-7)

Trademarks

Warning and Disclaimer

Dedication

With gratitude and appreciation to our three Millennial children, who require and expect much of their Boomer mother—an open mind, an unconditional heart, and, forever and always, another idea on career and life matters:

- Sarah, a Hebrew word meaning Princess, and that you are. May you always have a spirit to travel the world and learn from all people.

- Richard III, for three of a kind, although you are indeed an Original who one day soon will make a very fine Esquire.

- Tessa, you are and forever will be our greatest Asset, your name spelled backwards. May you continue to know the love of canines and felines everywhere you go.

And, most of all, to the Big Guy who stands beside me through sun and snow and rain and shine—thank you for choosing me to be the one for you.

To the hundreds upon hundreds of clients around the country who have taught me more than you'll ever know or imagine, I am truly grateful for the opportunity to serve you during your time of career transition and change. Thank you!

Acknowledgments

To Mitchell Levy, @*HappyAbout*, for his brilliant guidance in this newest adventure.

To Liz Tadman for her unwavering commitment to excellence on this Happy About project.

To Deneene Bell, copy editor, for her miraculous ability to perfect the written word.

To Jason Alba, @*JasonAlba*, for his amazing ability to be such an awe-inspiring link to so many and for his feedback and support.

To Ellie Halderman and Mrs. Cannon, two of my best teachers, for instilling in me that any story worth telling is worth telling well.

To Joyce Lain Kennedy, the dean of careers columnists and pioneer in the career development and management profession.

To Louise Fletcher, @*louise_fletcher*, Steve Gallison, @*SteveGallison*, Chris Perry, @*CareerRocketeer*, and Sital Ruparelia, @*SitalRuparelia*, for their advance reads and support.

A Message from Happy About®

Thank you for your purchase of this Happy About book. It is available online at http://www.happyabout.com/happyaboutcareeralphabet.php or at other online and physical bookstores.

- Please contact us for quantity discounts at sales@happyabout.info
- If you want to be informed by email of upcoming Happy About® books, please email bookupdate@happyabout.info

Happy About is interested in you if you are an author who would like to submit a non-fiction book proposal or a corporation that would like to have a book written for you. Please contact us by email editorial@happyabout.info or phone (1-408-257-3000).

Other Happy About books available include:

- I'm at a Networking Event—Now What???:
  http://www.happyabout.com/networking-event.php
- Internet Your Way to a New Job:
  http://happyabout.info/InternetYourWaytoaNewJob.php
- I Need to Brand My Story Online and Offline—Now What???:
  http://www.happyabout.com/ineeda-brandedbio.php
- Happy About My Resume:
  http://www.happyabout.com/myresume.php
- The Successful Introvert:
  http://happyabout.info/thesuccessfulintrovert.php
- I'm on LinkedIn—Now What???:
  http://happyabout.info/linkedinhelp.php
- I'm on Facebook—Now What???:
  http://happyabout.info/facebook.php
- Twitter Means Business:
  http://happyabout.info/twitter/tweet2success.php
- 42 Rules for Effective Connections:
  http://happyabout.info/42rules/effectiveconnections.php
- 42 Rules of Cold Calling Executives:
  http://www.happyabout.com/42rules/coldcallingexecutives.php
- 42 Rules™ to Jumpstart Your Professional Success:
  http://happyabout.info/42rules/jumpstartprofessionalservices.php
- Communicating the American Way:
  http://www.happyabout.com/communicating-american-way.php
- Happy About an Extra Hour Every Day:
  http://happyabout.info/an-extra-hour.php
- #MILLENNIALtweet Book01:
  http://www.happyabout.com/thinkaha/millennialtweet01.php

Contents

Foreword by Joyce Lain Kennedy

And I thought I was good at writing short-form advice to people seeking career lifts. Now I know I'm a piker compared to Billie Sucher, with her gift of concise, cogent guidance. You'll agree after reading the hundreds of her tweet-style messages of career-boosting wit and wisdom that grace these pages.

In this fast-paced era of tweeting and texting, the premise of this important book is especially compelling: less is more when sharing time-tested concepts and advice—with a full-throated salute to the future.

By sharing her best tips from a solid background of a master's degree in counseling and twenty-five years of consulting, counseling, and coaching, Billie nails it when she tells you how to develop the personal awareness and planning disciplines you need to master the twists and turns of your future.

Reflecting the finest tradition of brevity, Billie presents profound ideas in just a few words. You'll find many useful gems of thought here—clip those you like best or need to work on, and tape them to your mirror where they can do the most good in reminding you of smart moves and attitudes to surf this career world on your terms.

My alphabet letter for this book is "E" for excellent. If you can stand the pun, how tweet it is!

Joyce Lain Kennedy
Careers Columnist
Tribune Media Services

Introduction

Within these pages, you will find 800+ fast and easy tweet-style tips, thoughts, and ideas derived from twenty-five years of service in the career management trenches with clients from all walks of life, from all levels of the organization (entry to executive) and from all parts of the country. It has been my privilege to serve, counsel, learn, and share in the career successes of many. To all, thank you for the lessons and the learning that we have together known!

When I wrote my first career-related book, 'Between Jobs: Recover, Rethink, Rebuild,' over a decade ago, I wrote it using one-liners. Fast-forward to today and a new word called "tweets" has evolved into our vocabulary. Be it one-liners or tweets, may you find a good friend and career companion in 'Happy About The Career Alphabet.'

You can read one tweet per day, or, in less than sixty minutes, you can peruse the entire book and pick up tweet tips to last a lifetime! May you enjoy reading this book as much as I have enjoyed writing it for you. Somewhere buried within these pages, I hope you will discover a nugget or two that was written just for *you*!

And lastly, feel free to tell someone about this book via a text, a tweet, a blog post, a phone call, or a random mention in a face-to-face conversation. You just might make someone's search for a new beginning a little happier and a lot more hopeful! Happy reading and here's to *your* continued career success!

Billie Sucher, MS, CTMS, CTSB, JCTC, CCM
@billiesucher

P.S. I have intentionally left room at the back of the book for you to add your own tweet tips and job search reminders. If there's a particular tweet *you* would like to share, send it along to Happy About at http://happyabout.com/ for possible inclusion in a second edition.

A Abilities to Attitude to Awards

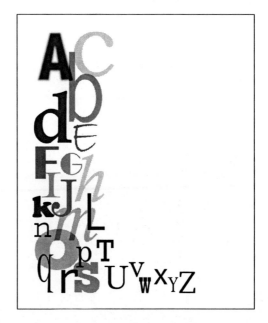

Abilities

Your abilities are your gifts that provide the potential to generate a lifelong income source to support your livelihood. What are yours?

Accept

Accept a job that you want, not one that you don't. Say *yes* to the opportunity that is right for you, and *no thanks* to the one that isn't.

Acceptance

Acceptance comes when you realize that the way it is now is simply the way it is. Like it or not, there's no going back to before.

Accomplishments

Career accomplishments are contributions you have made to the workplace during your professional life. Keep track—you'll be quizzed.

Accountable

You are accountable for each and every action, deed, and word affiliated with you, your name, and your brand.

Accountant

Verify with your accountant or the Internal Revenue Service what, if any, job search expenses can be deducted on your annual tax return.

Achievements

What are your five best achievements in the past one, three, five years? Know with quantifiable precision—you'll be asked time and again.

Act

Act with consistency in all that you do, and do not use, abuse, or take advantage of any person in your network.

Action

Stop talking about it, and start taking action NOW—don't wait for the tomorrows of your life.

Action Steps

Action steps mean the difference between getting somewhere and going nowhere.

Action Verbs

Use action verbs to create a résumé that will wow the reader to action! Avoid repetition by doing a Google search of "résumé action words."

Active

Keep yourself active mentally and physically to create your very best self. It takes a vast amount of positive energy to find a new job!

Adaptability

Adaptability is a trait that allows you to readily embrace the ever-changing needs and demands of today's global workplace.

Adjectives

What five adjectives best describe Brand You? For job-related descriptors, research online at http://www.onetonline.org/.

Advancement

Advancement comes in many forms: up, down, sideways, backward, and forward. The point is to keep learning and growing regardless.

Advantage

What is your competitive advantage? Name five ways you outshine your competition. What can you deliver that your competition can't?

Advertisement

You are your own best advertisement. First, figure out what you are selling—the product you—before you ever go to market.

Advice

Advice comes with consequences. So before you take good (or bad) advice to heart, consider the credibility of the source.

Advise

Advise your network about the type of job you want. Offer specificity to generate spot-on leads that align with your target goals.

Advisory

Build an advisory team to help you succeed in your career and professional life. Be bold and courageous in seeking guidance and direction.

Advocate

Advocacy starts and ends with you. Stand up for yourself, speak up on your own behalf, and become your own best advocate.

Affirmations

Positive affirmations are the motivational and inspirational words you keep telling yourself and others to maximize job search momentum.

Age

Age is a number that works for you or against you. Is your age working for you, or is it the excuse that's holding you back?

Agencies

Contact a variety of employment firms: recruiters, state reemployment centers, and temporary placement firms to glean ideas and information.

Aggressive

Are you appropriately aggressive in pursuing your goals and dreams? What, if anything, can you do today to inch closer to your goals?

Agreement

Before you sign a legally binding document, read the fine print. Know what you're agreeing to before you agree to it.

Alignment

Is there a good fit between you and the job you desire? The more the two are aligned, the greater your chances of success and happiness.

All

Can you have it all? Before you answer that, first figure out your definition of "all," and then you'll know if you can or not.

Alternative

If one thing isn't working in your job search, try another. Always have a back-up Plan B, Plan C, and Plan D.

Alumni

Connect with your college alumni office to enlist their thoughts, ideas, and support with your job search and career goals.

Ambassador

Always strive to be an exemplary ambassador to others, be it an employer, your community, or a person whose life you touch.

Ambition

Let others know of your ambition and goals and invite them to mentor you, guide you, and support you in the process.

Americans with Disabilities Act (ADA)

Know your rights and it may well keep you from many wrongs.

Analyze

Analyze a job offer for duties, resources, expectations, location, hours, salary, vacation, benefits, bonus, and incentives.

Antennae

Always have your antennae up and on—you may discover a contact, piece of information, or idea worth sharing with a friend or colleague.

Anticipate

Anticipate questions you may be asked in an interview. Stay calm, focus, take a moment to formulate a good answer, and then respond.

Appearance

You get one chance to shine at an interview. Always dazzle your audience with these three Ps: professionalism, positivity, preparedness.

Application

When completing an employment application online, follow directions. If filling out by hand, use black ink and print, don't handwrite.

Appropriate

Being appropriate counts when it comes to appearance, attitude, attire, and actions before, during, and after the interview.

Area Code

When leaving a voice message, speak clearly so your message, including your callback number with area code, can be easily understood.

Arrogance

There is a fine line between confidence and arrogance—one will help you and the other will hurt you and your career.

ASCII (American Standard Code for Information Interchange)

When you need to create and save your résumé in different formats (ASCII, web-based, PDF, MS Word) go here: http://www.asciiresume.com.

Ask

Ask for what you want. Ask for what you need. Ask for help. Ask when you don't know. Ask questions—lots of them—until you get answers.

Aspiration

Aspiration trumps imagination, for without it you having nothing but a notion.

Assessments

If you're unclear about career options, take a career assessment, online or offline. Search Google or Bing for "career assessments."

Assets

You're born with many assets, talents, and abilities—the trick is to know what they are and share them with others. What are yours?

Associate

Be selective about the words you associate with you and your brand. Make the thesaurus your friend and use words that match your message.

Assumptions

Assumptions are just that. Whatever it is you're wondering about, get the facts from a credible source. Make no assumptions!

Attainable

Are your goals, dreams, and desires attainable? How do you plan to achieve them?

Attire

Keep your career attire appropriate, even in casual work environments. From top to toe, make it your professional best! People notice.

Attitude

The best credentials in the world won't outshine a poor attitude. How will others describe your attitude?

Attorney

Seek the legal counsel of a competent employment law "expert" when dealing with career-related contracts and issues.

Attraction

Are people naturally and easily drawn to you and is it easy, or difficult, for you to gain attraction for your brand?

Attributes

Name five words that well describe you and your attributes. Avoid using commonly cited words such as loyal, honest, and hardworking.

Authenticity

Do you present yourself to the world as genuine, real, and authentic? Name one strategy you employ to show the world your authenticity.

Awards

During your employment in the past three to five years, what awards have you received from your employer, or civic, or professional groups?

B Baby Boomer to Black Hole to Business Card

Baby Boomer

If you were born between 1946 and 1964, you are known as a Baby Boomer.

Bad Habits

Bad habits are yours to convert to best practices. What, if any, are your bad habits and what action steps can you take to rectify them?

Bad-Mouth

Do not bad-mouth your current or past employers, colleagues, or customers. The one it hurts the most is you!

Baggage

Transition with grace, confidence, and style. Let go of any baggage you may harbor toward yourself or someone else.

Balance

Find balance in your personal and professional life. You will be happier and your life will be more satisfying, fulfilling, and rewarding.

Basics

Focus on these six Ss of interview basics: suit, shirt, socks, shoes, smile, and scents to produce the best chance for success!

Be

Be the best at whatever it is you choose to pursue and do. To do otherwise is to do a great disservice to yourself and others.

Become

Become a subject-matter expert in something and then let others know what that is in fewer than ten words.

Before

Who were you before you got to be who you are now? What, if anything, do you need to get back to, to be yourself once again?

Beginning

You can always start over, even though you might think otherwise. Each new day brings another chance to begin anew. Take the plunge!

Behavioral Interviewing

Behavioral interviewing affords an opportunity to share examples and stories to support your candidacy for a position. (*Tell me a story...*)

Believability

Do you exude believability in all things you say and do?
#personalbranding

Believe in Yourself

Believe in yourself. If you don't, you will have a tough time convincing a hiring manager that you're the best candidate for the job.

Benefits

Inquire about employment benefits only when an offer has been extended to you. Doing so beforehand sends the wrong message.

Best Practices

What best practices, if any, have you integrated into your job search? Have they proven to be of value for you? What needs more work?

Bilingual

If you're bilingual or multilingual, be sure to include the specific language(s) you speak fluently in the body of your résumé.

Billboard

Create a billboard advertisement about yourself. What's your brand message? What's your value? Does your ad sound credible and compelling?

Bing

Bing yourself weekly. Know what others are saying about you and what's posted on the Internet about you. (*#no surprises*)

Black Hole

There will be times when you feel like you're pouring your resources, energy, and time into a black hole; it goes with today's job search.

Blame

Blame no one for your career situation or circumstance, as it will only exhaust you and distract you from getting on with your life.

Blather

Less is more. In conversation, watch out for blather—yours and theirs—blah, blah, blah. Think Twitter: 140 characters or less.

Blind Date

At an interview, you're there for one purpose: to determine if your blind date will warrant a second meeting or a marriage proposal.

Blog

Start a blog. If you don't want to start your own, identify guest blogging opportunities. Freely give of your passion and knowledge.

Blogging

Blogging is an effective way to build your online brand, share your expertise and find your voice in cyberspace.

Blueprint

Develop your blueprint for career success. Define in detail the elements of work you would love. First focus, then seek and find.

Body Language

Let your body language convey a message of confidence in your interactions and exchanges with others.

Boring

If you think your résumé is boring and if you think you are "bad" at interviewing, you are probably right. Do yourself a favor: *#get #help*.

Boss

Work for someone who supports you. No support = no success. It's that simple.

Bottom Line

Name five specific ways you will contribute to an organization's bottom line. Ask yourself, are these things important to them or to me?

Bounce Back

Things will not always go your way—you will be tried, you will be tested. You will also discover the substance of which you are made.

Brag Book

Keep a running log of your projects, successes, and achievements. As the days and months progress, you can readily measure results.

Brand

Know your brand before you seek new career opportunities. Your brand is the thing people will remember you by—in five words or less.

Brand Alignment

When what you're looking for and what they're looking for is of mutual value, it then creates a good partnership and brand alignment.

Brand Benefit

What benefit will your brand deliver to a prospective employer? Be able to articulate this before you interview! *#branding #competition*

Brand Promise

Brand promise is delivering what you say you will, when you say you will, and how you say you will—today, tomorrow, and always. *#consistent*

Break

Break habits that don't serve you well. Break out of old ways that don't work. Break down barriers to build a brighter future.

Bs of Business

Consider the three Bs of career options: buy, build, or be in a business as an employee or contractor. All have pros and cons.

Build

Build lasting, mutually beneficial relationships rooted in mutual like, trust, and respect.

Building Blocks

The building blocks of your future are taking shape each and every day, whether you're paying attention or not.

Business Card

Carry your own (not your current or most recent employer's) business card 24/7 when you're looking for work. It's expected.

C Calculators to Curriculum Vitae

Calculators

Research at least three online "salary calculators" to establish a competitive price for your talent and skill set. (#pay calculators)

Call

When you lose your job, call someone who cares, who will listen unconditionally, and who is invested in your well-being—no strings attached.

Calling

When you know without hesitation or reservation that you are doing exactly what you were intended to do, that then is your calling.

Calm

Stay calm amidst chaos; you will distinguish yourself from the crowd in a volatile and turbulent global marketplace.

Can

Can-do paves the way to anything, everything, and something. It is a way of thinking and a way of life—yours to embrace if you choose.

Candidate

As a job candidate, put your best foot forward and deliver the presentation of a lifetime. This is your one chance to shine—make it count!

Can't

"Can't" is a surefire way to nothing, nowhere, and no one. It has a way of stopping and sabotaging you each and every step of the way.

Capitalize

Remember, you get to keep your knowledge when you lose your job; no one can take it from you. Leverage what you know.

Card

Ask the hiring manager for a business card when you interview. Then, write and send a typed thank you note within twenty-four hours.

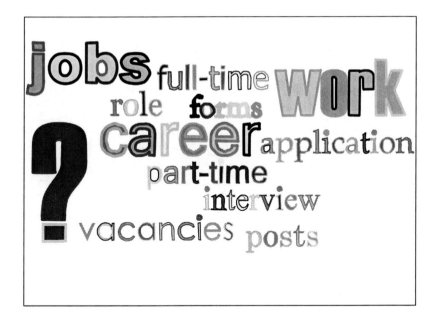

Career

Choose a career that is a good and right fit for you—regardless of how much your family, friends, and advisors try to sway or influence you.

Career Coach

Before you fork over your hard-earned money to a "coach," be sure they have more expertise than you do! Ask the tough questions!

Career Counselor

Find a competent career counselor or career management professional with whom you click. Otherwise, you are wasting your time and money.

Career Hub

Career Hub, http://www.careerhubblog.com, is a top-ranked career-related blog on the Internet. It offers "free advice from career experts."

Caring

Genuinely caring about the success, well-being, and happiness of others will make you stand out in today's workplace.

Carriage

How you carry yourself (your carriage) sends a message to the hiring manager. Walk with head high, back straight, and chin up.

Caught

Don't be caught off guard by someone who thinks they know more about you than you know about yourself.

CEO

As Creator of Entrepreneurial Options (CEO), what can you create to provide income and opportunity for yourself?

Certification

What certifications, if any, would make you a more attractive and competitive candidate in the eyes of a hiring manager or recruiter?

Challenges

Prior to an interview, identify potential challenges regarding your candidacy and develop strategies to optimize your position.

Chance

When you get a chance, take it—and don't mess it up!

Change

Change is something to reckon with on a daily basis in today's job search climate. Face it, don't fear it, and find your way through it.

Character

How would you best describe your character? What would your immediate supervisor say? What would your colleagues and customers say?

Characteristics

What characteristics do you find most valuable about yourself? What, if any, do you need to improve?

Charisma

Charisma is that "wow factor" that gives you an edge over the person seated next to you. Do you have charisma, and why or why not?

Choices

Don't make career choices before you have to. Gather all the facts, and then decide.

Clarification

When you are asked a question you don't understand or are directed to do something you are uncertain about, get clarification before acting.

Clarify

Clarify and verify everything as you move through your job search.

Clarity

The greater the clarity in identifying your career goals, the greater the likelihood of achievement.

Classroom

In job search, your classroom becomes anyplace where you learn something of value, be it in a coffee shop, a club, or a conference room.

Cleanliness

Cleanliness is imperative when you're looking for employment—from top to toe, clean hair, body, clothes, fingernails and shoes.

Clever

Consider all clever, appropriate, and ingenious ideas and strategies possible in solving the mystery of finding a new job.

Cold Calling

Cold calling both online and offline goes with job search. You don't have to like it; you just need to do it until the next job is found.

Colleagues

Your colleagues have an opinion of you—what is it?

College

Contact your college career office and inquire about the services, if any, they can provide to help you with your career transition.

Cologne

Keep cologne to a minimum. Some people are allergic to fragrances, and you don't want to be remembered by how you smell.

Commensurate

Is your salary commensurate with your skill level? Why or why not? Conduct research to determine your current market value.

Commitment

The commitment you make to the job-hunt process conveys much to potential employers about the type of employee they will be acquiring.

Common Sense

Use good, old-fashioned common sense not only in your career life but in all facets of your life, to help you make sound decisions.

Communication

Join Toastmasters International if you are not a confident speaker; it will change your life in multiple ways! http://www.toastmasters.org.

Community

What do you do to share your gifts and talents and give back to members of your community on a volunteer basis?

Community College

Contact a community college near you and inquire about "free" or "low cost" career assessments to help with career planning activities.

Compensation

Compensation embodies a number of factors: salary, benefits (vacation, personal time, health insurance), and other possible perks.

Competent

Be enormously competent in all that you undertake; it will distinguish you time and again.

Competition

Competition will motivate and inspire you or stymie and stop you. Only you can choose to stand still or stand up and stand out.

Compliance

Adhere to the employer's request for résumé and materials submission. To do otherwise suggests you can't (or won't) follow directions.

Concerns

Listen carefully for the word "concern" as the interview progresses. It is your chance to overcome objections about your candidacy.

Concise

When you write or speak, remember to think Twitter: 140 characters or less.

Confidence

Confidence—if you don't have it, get it. And if you don't know how to get it, ask somebody who's got it.

Confidential

Protect and preserve confidential information; do not share proprietary data, sensitive materials, or trade secrets. Shhh!

Confirm

Confirm the date, time, and location prior to attending a meeting with another party. Verify street addresses with a human being, not a GPS.

Confusion

Looking for a job can be confusing, especially when you don't know the rules of the game. Get help from a competent pro.

Connect

Connect with others through various online social networking sites such as LinkedIn, Twitter, and Facebook.

Connections

Build, value, and sustain your connections! In job search, your network can be your eyes and ears to the next new opportunity. *#diversify*

Consequences

For each and every career choice you make, you will reap the consequences, both good and not so good—your call.

Consideration

Give deliberate and thoughtful consideration to employment offers. Do not sign papers or agree to terms on the spot or under duress.

Consistency

Do you demonstrate consistency in all that you do and say and in how you present yourself to others? *#brand #consistency*

Constructive

Make a list of 25 constructive and positive coping mechanisms you can call upon to effectively manage this interim period of unemployment.

Contact

Verify contact info on all career marketing materials. Include telephone area code and number, address, email, LinkedIn and Twitter URLs.

Contacts

Stay in touch with your contacts in both good and bad times. People have long memories and will remember if they feel used by you.

Continuous Improvement

What initiatives have you implemented into your job search process to make it better, easier, and faster to achieve your desired goals?

Contracts

Getting into an employment contract is much less complicated (and costly) than getting out of one! Secure a legal review before signing.

Control

What parts of your job search are fully within your control? Evaluate to see if you are controlling the elements within your power to do so.

Conversations

Little words like "hi," "hey," and "sup" can lead to conversations that yield a lifetime of friendship.

Conviction

Do you pursue your passions with conviction, energy, and enthusiasm? Why or why not?

Cooperation

Do you have a spirit of cooperation and teamwork? In what ways do you demonstrate these qualities in the workplace?

Coping

What coping skills are you relying upon to see you through this challenging period of unemployment? Are they constructive or destructive?

Core Competencies

Core competencies are your best, most preferred gifts, talents, and abilities that you offer an organization to support its vision and goals.

Cost

Will you make the employer money or cost the employer money? Will you generate a good return on investment or will you be a risk?

Course

A change in course often leads to greater satisfaction, happiness, and fulfillment (even though you may not think so at the time).

Courtesy

Be as courteous to the front-desk receptionist as you are to the President/CEO. You will stand out and it may get you hired!

Cover Letter

A cover letter is like a good speech; it has a clear, concise opening, body, and closing, Keep content relevant to your job target.

Creativity

Creativity has more to do with your thinking ability than your drawing skills; it will help you stand out as an original, not a carbon copy.

Credibility

Credibility is yours to gain and yours to lose. You can spend a lifetime building it, but with one bad decision you can ruin it forever.

Criminal Record

Speak with an employment attorney if you have a criminal record. They can help you determine what to do before you begin your job search.

Cultivate

Cultivate relationships if you expect them to blossom.

Cultural

Make yourself aware of other cultures, customs, and practices to stand out in an interview. You are not the only person on the planet.

Curiosity

Curiosity is the seed that sows new insights, innovations, and ideas. What are you curious about?

Curriculum Vitae

A CV is a written account of experience, education, and skills, often used in academic and medical settings. *#international*

D Dare to Discipline to DUI

Dare

Dare to do something that will stretch you and make you a better person than you are today.

Deal

Ask questions before the deal is done, not after when it's too late! It will save you time, money, headache, and heartache.

Decide

Sometimes you just decide that taking any action is better than taking no action to move closer to your target goal.

Decisions

Do thorough and complete homework, research, and due diligence before arriving at your decision. *#careers #jobs*

Degree

You either have a degree or you don't, and you will either get one or you won't.

Deliver

If you were asked to cite three things you are known for delivering to the workplace, what three items would be on your list?

Demeanor

How would others describe your professional demeanor?

Demons

Discover any digital-dirt demons prior to your interview, not during or after! Do your best to bury them on "page 15" of a Google search!

Depression

If depression is controlling your life, immediately seek the services of a licensed mental health care professional. Do not delay!

Description

Read the job description first before applying for a job. Then, target your résumé to meet the specific needs of the employer.

Desire

Your desire is an indicator of how badly you want something and what you are willing to sacrifice to get it.

Desperation

What would happen if you replaced desperation with inspiration?

Destination

Do not get derailed en route to your career destination by buying in to gloom and doom, marketplace negativity, and economic doldrums.

Details

Details matter. They help you remember a conversation, a name, or a deed that can connect you for a lifetime. Details can decide your fate.

Detective

Looking for a job? Think like a detective. Be a good sleuth. Listen. Observe. Notice. Ask. Discover. Explore. Dig until you solve the case.

Determination

The amount of determination you have within you is what will separate you from your competition. How determined are you?

Digital Dirt

Digital dirt is what others will use to rule out your candidacy for an opportunity. Know what is being said about you, online and offline.

Direction

In what direction is your career taking you? Are you happy with the direction or is now the time to turn around and make some changes?

Disability

Focus on what you can do, not what you can't do. Discuss your "ability" not your "dis"ability. *#networking #interviewing*

Discipline

Regardless of the occupation you pursue, it will require extreme discipline and focus on your part to find it. Don't get derailed.

Discouraged

On the days you are discouraged in your quest to find a job, make a list of items for which you are grateful and thankful.

Discover

Discover new employment opportunities by meeting people, asking questions, and maintaining a positive outlook as you explore options.

Discretion

Use your discretion and keep personal things private at professional interviews or networking events; don't share personal drama or trauma.

Discrimination

In what ways, if any, have you experienced discrimination in your job search? Has it stopped you or spurred you on?

Distinctive

What makes you—the job seeker—distinctive? Cite three ways in which your brand stands out from the crowd. Don't interview until you know!

Distractions

At interviews, do not let little things become distractions (e.g., chewing gum, nail biting, answering your phone, interrupting, fidgeting).

Documents

Essential career marketing documents: business card, résumé, references, LinkedIn profile with a minimum of ten recommendations.

Dollars

Fill in the space below with the salary range you seek: $_____ to _____. Is this range fair and competitive in today's market?

Down

Don't look back. Don't look down. Onward and upward, starting now!

Downsized

What, if anything, have you learned from losing your job? What have been the greatest benefits of being downsized?

Dreams

Before you got to be who, where, what, and how you are now, what were your dreams? Have you fulfilled them? Why or why not?

Drive

How would you best describe the amount of drive you have when it comes to exploring a new opportunity?

Driver

Regardless of what the market and economy is or isn't doing, you are in the driver's seat. You are in charge of you! Are you a good driver?

Due Diligence

Before making important decisions about a job or business acquisition, conduct extensive due diligence; you'll thank yourself later.

DUI (Driving Under the Influence)/DWI (Driving While Intoxicated)

If you are the recipient of a DUI/DWI, contact a legal expert who can direct you on what to do or not do regarding this legal matter. *#smart*

E | Easy to Engaging to Eyes

Easy

If you think looking for a job is easy, talk with a person who's lost theirs. You will soon discover that today's job search is like no other.

Educate

Educate the hiring manager about you and your features, value, and benefit as you align your credentials with the organization's needs.

Education

Learn all that you can, whenever you can, however you can, to better serve yourself and others. Focus on what you have, not what you don't!

Eligible

Offer to an employer, before being asked, why you are eligible for a new job. In other words, why are you a free agent at this time?

Email

Create an email address used specifically for your job search; make it appropriate, easy to read, simple, and, preferably, your own name.

Employee Traits

Employee traits are the unique qualities that make you *you*. Identify five traits that support your target goal in the employer's eyes.

Employer

The employer wants to know if you will make the company money or cost the company money—which one will you do and why?

Employment

Explore employment opportunities that are a good fit with you, your preferences, your interests, and your values. You'll be happier.

Employment Agency

An employment agency may or may not help you find a job. Identify fee-paid only firms of no cost to you. Keep your money in your pocket!

Ending

When you lost your job, what ended for you? Make a list to see what to let go of, give up, give back, or get back.

Endorsement

Invite your references to write you an endorsement/recommendation to use in your résumé. Keep it brief and aligned with the new job target.

Energy

The energy you communicate in an interview tells the employer much about you—do you act lively and with-it or dull and disinterested?

Engaging

Will hiring managers view you as an engaging or disengaging candidate? What, if anything, can you do to enhance this Brand You element?

Enthusiasm

What interests you? What excites you? What are you passionate about? Can others detect your enthusiasm?

Entrepreneur

An entrepreneur says "why not?" and doesn't focus on failure. He/she "gets" that success means various forms of sweat and proceeds anyway.

Entrepreneurial

Prerequisites for an entrepreneur: What business will you start? What risks will you take? What are you willing to sacrifice or lose?

Environment

What surroundings are must-haves in your preferred work environment? Decide what's important before accepting an offer.
#job #satisfaction

Equality

View yourself as an equal partner in conversations with hiring managers, recruiters, and your network. #partnership

Equity

How much equity do you have in the product you? What would you say if an employer asked you this question?

Essence

In ten words or less, how would you best describe the true essence of Brand You? Know this before you go to market!

Essential

What are the basic elements you seek in a job? Once you determine the necessities, identify opportunities embodying those elements.

Ethics

What ethics, principles, and practices guide your day-to-day work life?

Evaluate

Evaluate your interview performance: What did you learn? What, if anything, can you improve? What's the next step in the process?

Evaluation

No matter where you go, no matter what you do, someone, somewhere, will be performing an evaluation of you and your brand.

Evidence

What direct evidence can you offer an employer to prove that you have what it takes to do the job at hand and win your case for employment?

Excellence

Everything you say and do is a reflection of you—are you committed to excellence in today's continuous improvement environment?

Exception

Look for the exception in each possibility; maybe the employer required a college degree until they met you, the person without one!

Excuses

Are you an excuse-maker? Do you make excuses for where you are, or aren't, in your career? What is your excuse now?

Exemplify

Exemplify excellence and energy and serve as an example to each and every person you meet in your professional and personal life.

Exercise

There are multiple opportunities to keep fit physically, emotionally, socially, and intellectually. What exercise matters to you?

Expedition

Please cite three reasons why you have ceased your job-search hunting expedition, if you have:
1.
2.
3.

Expenses

Keep track of monies you invest in your career transition. Keep a file (online or offline) delineating every cent spent on the process.

Experience

Experience is built through a series of choices and consequences that only you can make, day after day, hour after hour, moment by moment.

Experiment

You may try on several different jobs before you find one that is a good fit for you. Learn from your experiments.

Expert

Become very good at something and share your expertise! If you can't figure out what you're naturally good at, invite others to tell you!

Exploration

Take time to research and investigate opportunities of potential interest before you make important career decisions.

Eye Contact

In conversation with another person, one way to connect is through eye contact. Look directly into the person's eyes without staring.

Eyes

Your eyes say everything without saying anything.

Face to Fundamentals

Face

Face it—whatever it is—head on.

Fact Finding

An informational interview is a fact-finding expedition and bears no "yes" or "no" outcome, as does employment interviewing. *#wisdom*

Failure

Failure is a word, not a way of life. Failure gives you a chance to learn and apply lessons learned to next time's adventure.

Faith

Faith makes possible the impossible.

Fake

Employers can spot a fake within seconds. Project your best real, genuine, and authentic self! Be the one candidate they remember! *#brand*

Familiar

Become familiar with social media tools and resources such as blogging, LinkedIn and Twitter to publicize, promote, and support Brand You.

Family

Family is your first and finest network when things go wrong and when things go right.

Favorite

What are five favorite skills you would prefer to use to earning a living? Name them. Are you presently using them? Why? Why not?

Fear

Fear holds you back. Fear keeps you stuck. Fear also moves you forward and helps you find your way. Which way is fear driving your career?

Feedback

What will your current or most recent "boss" say you need to work on? What steps have you taken to address this problem area?

Feelings

Pay attention to both good and bad gut feelings about a professional opportunity. What warning signs and red flags, if any, can you detect?

Fees

When purchasing career management services, clarify fees, terms, conditions, and refunds, if any. Get recommendations. *#predatory*

Field

Seek employment in a field you are generally interested in. You will have a better chance at being happy and finding fulfillment.

Fill in the Blanks

I'd like a job in the _____ industry where my experience in _____,

_____ and _____ contributes to an organization's _____.

Filter

Filter incoming data when people start telling you what you can't do instead of what you can do. Smile and continue on life's journey.

Financial Advisor

Seek the professional services of a competent financial advisor if you are unable to figure out finances on your own.

Financial Position

When you lose your job, immediately assess your financial situation to determine your financial position and areas for reduced spending.

Find

Find work that you enjoy more than you dislike. It's that simple and that complicated.

Finish

Whatever the goal, if it means something to you, stay focused until you cross the finish line. Put fear and discouragement on the sidelines.

Fired

If and when you get fired, you will be fine. Just keep telling yourself that until you realize that you really are going to be okay!

First Impressions

When you get the chance, deliver your best performance; there are no "do-overs" in life.

First Step

The first step for me right now is: _____.

Fit

On paper and in person, you may have the most talent; in reality, the employer strives to find the best fit!

Fitness

Commit to fitness: physical, emotional, spiritual, financial, and professional. You'll be happier and so will everyone else around you!

Five

What are five words that best describe you as a worker? (Please do not say loyal, honest, hardworking, or dependable; they've been said!)

Focus

What job will make you happy? Instead of saying "I don't know" or "I'll take anything," do yourself a big favor—get specific.

Follow Up

Follow up and follow through; you will distinguish yourself from your competition with this consistent habit of excellence.

Forget

Forget about what might have been and figure out what might be.

Forgive

Forgive yourself. Forgive him. Forgive her. Then focus more on the second syllable "give" than on the first.

Forgiveness

Forgiveness can be a life-changing event. Is there anyone in your world you need to forgive? What about forgiving yourself?

Format

Three common résumé formats: chronological, combination, and functional. Use the format that best aligns your brand with the job target.

Formula

What's your formula for success? If you don't have one, write your formula for failure, then do the exact opposite.

Foster

Foster friendships by freely sharing resources, ideas, and insights. Stay in touch, not just in tough times or rough spots.

Found

If you can't be found online via a Google search, build an online presence to level the playing field with your competition, who will.

Fragrances

Fragrances, for some, are troublesome and toxic. If someone can smell you before they see you, you've overdone it! A dab will do.

Free Agent

Briefly explain why you're a free agent; don't make the hiring manager drag it out of you. Say why you're in transition then stop talking.

Freelancing

Consider freelancing, self-employment, and/or independent contracting. Think: Me, Inc. Think: You, Inc. Think: Brand You CEO.

Friendliness

Is your demeanor one of friendliness and approachability or are you distant and aloof in your conversation and presentation?

Friends

If people you thought were your friends disappear when you lose a job, maybe they don't know what to say or what to do. Call them!

Frustration

One of two things will happen with job search frustration: it will manage you, or you will manage it.

Fun

Routinely ask yourself these questions as you explore new opportunities: Am I having fun? Is this fun? Am I fun?

Fundamentals

A-job-hunting-you-will-go does not begin until you have mastered the basic fundamentals of how to look for work in today's job market.

Game to Gut

Game

Don't take yourself out of the job search game when you don't need to.

Gather

Gather information, including salary data, from online salary calculators, recruiters, colleagues, and professional associations. *#research*

Generation

Regardless of your generation—Millennial, Gen X, Baby Boomer or Traditionalist—you have much to share and much to learn! *#workplace*

Genius

Genius comes in many shapes, styles, forms, and ways. What genius lies within you?

Genuine

Let others see, know, experience, and understand the genuine you. And that will be enough.

Geography

Live in a geographical area that brings you more joy than misery.

Get It

Do you "get it"? If you do, what, exactly do you get? If you don't, what do you need to get?

Get Noticed

Align your résumé and cover letter text with the employer's needs to maximize your chances of getting noticed by the hiring manager.

Give

What do you willfully, freely, and easily give to others, without condition and without a "what's in it for me" mentality?

Giving

Giving is what you do because you choose to, not because you have to.

Giving Up

Giving up is not an option—ever! Do not give up looking for a job. Dig deep; find that extra special something within you to keep going!

Glances

When a stranger glances at your résumé, in five to eight seconds, can they discern what you want to do with evidence of why you can do it?

Global

Do you have a global perspective? How would you respond to this question if asked during a job interview?

Goals

What are five of your most important short-term and long-term goals? Have you set realistic time frames to achieve these goals?

Good

Whatever it is you decide to do, be really good at it and you will always have work.

Goodness

How do you seek and find the goodness in others?

Google

Google your name. What will you (or the hiring manager) find, if anything, to diminish and/or increase your candidacy for the position?

Grateful

Make a list of five things for which you are truly grateful.

Gratitude

Do you exhibit an attitude of gratitude, appreciation, and thankfulness for the abundance in your life? Why or why not?

Grit

Grit is a gift in both good and trying times. It keeps you going when nothing else will.

Grounded

Would others describe your character as someone who is well grounded? Why or why not?

Guest

When dining at a job interview, if the check is placed in front of you, ignore it; do not touch or stare at it, you are the guest of honor.

Gut

Gut feelings deserve your notice. Pay attention. Listen to them. What, if anything, are they telling you about the job you're considering?

H Habits to Help to Hurdles

Habits

What are your best work habits? What work habits have others recommended as areas needing improvement?

Handicaps

Handicaps hold us back and propel us forward. Only you can decide which direction you'll go. Keep telling yourself you can! *#You can do it!*

Hands

When someone sees your hands, what conclusions might they draw about you?

Handshake

Your handshake can buy you a job offer or get you booted. Practice your handshake to deliver it with comfort and confidence.
#wimpy no more

Happiness

Happiness is a by-product of making choices that are a good fit with you, who you are, your preferences, likes, dislikes. Are you happy?

Happy About

What are you happy about? This is always a good question to consider as you are exploring your career options! *#gratitude #thankfulness*

Have

Have skills will travel. Your security lies within you; no one but you and you alone can make you feel secure in today's chaotic workplace.

Heal

When you lose your job, take the first few hours and/or days to heal your wounds, even if it takes maximum-strength mental Band-Aids.

Health

Preserve and protect a healthy lifestyle as you explore new employment opportunities.

Heart

Are you working from your heart or can you barely find a pulse for the work you are now doing?

Hello

A simple hello can serve as a catalyst to new information, new people, and new opportunity. H-E-L-L-O—five characters to a changed life!

Help

"I need your help": four of the easiest and most difficult words known to humankind.

Helpfulness

Helpfulness comes with no expectations, no conditions, and no paybacks. When you help others succeed, you'll be more successful!

Hindrance

What is your biggest hindrance to achieving your professional goals? What, if anything, can you do to alleviate it?

Hint

Think like the hiring manager thinks during the interview process: state only relevant, evidence-based content in support of your candidacy.

Hired

Music to a job seeker's ears: "You're hired!" And when you hear such words, it's your cue that the job hunt is over—for now.

Hiring

Hiring is a process toward partnership, one that takes time and patience on both the employer's and job seeker's part. Both want the best!

Hiring Manager

The easier you make the hiring manager's job, the greater your chances of standing out in his or her eyes. Help your case, don't hurt it!

Homework

Remember when your teachers said, "Do your homework"? Job search is a good time to heed their words!

Honesty

Honesty is a choice. Choose wisely.

Hope

What does hope mean to you? Do you feel hopeful or hopeless? What would you tell your friend to do to feel hopeful? (Apply it to yourself!)

Hours

How many hours until you find a new job? Record the time spent per day, week, and month on this project; are you on schedule?

How

How you go about looking for work makes all the difference in potential earnings, length of search, and how you're perceived by the employer.

How Come

How come you're unemployed? If you're so great, how come you're still jobless? HR will want to know. Plot your answer before your interview.

How Many of Me

Go to http://www.howmanyofme.com for the best way to list your name in cyberspace and avoid confusion with another person of the same name.

How Much

How much money will it take to hire you? If you don't know your product's dollar value, then you're not ready to go to market. *#research*

Human Resources (HR)

Your future, in part, starts and ends with the HR Department. Even if you circumvent HR now, you will wind up there later. Be nice!

Hungry

If you are hungry, you will hunt for a job and remain unfazed by the economy, the elements, or the self-imposed excuses.

Hunter

A hunter hunts and doesn't stop hunting. If you're unemployed, have you stopped looking for work? Yes? No? Why? Why not?

Hurdles

There will be many hurdles to address during your career, including the one you may be facing right now which is…?

I | Ideal to Investment

Ideal

The ideal job for me would be a job where I...

Ideas

One of the best ideas I ever had for a career was _____. If you can't think of ideas for yourself, what ideas would you offer your friend?

Identification

Identification of your knowledge, skills, and abilities (KSA) is a key starting point in determining what's next in your career path.

Identify

Identify opportunities of interest. Choose at least three target options to thoroughly research and explore in the coming days:
1.
2.
3.

Identity

Your job is important but is only a job. Do not let it become your sole identity, so if and when you lose it, you'll still know who you are.

If

If you don't know what you want, then what *don't* you want? (Do the opposite of that to discover what you want).

Ignore

Ignore advice that some people will give you; bad advice is worse than no advice. In one ear and out the other! Done and done!

Illegal

Illegal and/or inappropriate questions may be asked of you during the interview. Manage your responses in a calm, professional manner.

Imagination

Imagination is the magical ingredient that allows you to move forward when everyone else around you is in a quandary and a state of flux.

Imagine

Imagine all of the possibilities to pursue by making a short list of those most interesting to you. What options are on your list?

Impression

You get to choose the impression you make and the memory that others take away about you. What do you wish that memory to be?

Income

Develop various ways to generate income; that way, when one source dries up, you're still in business, thanks to multiple revenue streams.

Inference

If using an email address other than your own name, select one where no inference can be made; support your professional brand image!

Information

Make critical career and life decisions based on truthful, factual information instead of hearsay, rumor, and speculation.

Informational Interviewing

Informational interviewing lets you learn more about an opportunity and ask who, what, when, where, why, how, how-much questions.

Initiative

Initiative separates you from the next person. It's the drive, the gumption, the giddy-up within you to go on without being told to do so.

Instincts

Trust your instincts; if something doesn't feel right, look right, sound right, or smell right, don't do it, no matter what anyone else says.

Integrate

Integrate existing business savvy into your job search. Apply common business practices and principles you've used before to build a career.

Integrity

You can spend a lifetime showing others that you have integrity; however, with one wrong move, it can be stripped from you in seconds.

Intellect

Share what you know, not what you don't. Don't belittle yourself (or others) as it diminishes the power and credibility of you, your brand.

Intelligent

What matters isn't how intelligent you are; what matters is how are you smart and how can you use that intellect to serve self and others?

Interested

If you are interested in a particular opportunity, let the decision-maker know it's exactly what you're looking for: "I'd love this job!"

Interesting

Are you an interesting person? Yes? No? If you're not interesting, will a prospective employer be interested in you?

Interests

What are your interests at this time in your life? What, if any, bearing will they have upon your future career choices and preferences?

International

List international travel, internships, and both paid and unpaid work experience in your résumé or curriculum vitae. Share your global experience.

Internet

The Internet is both friend and foe in your job search. Don't let it overshadow opportunities to connect face-to-face with your contacts!

Internship

Actively pursue internship opportunities at home or abroad to expand your knowledge base. Paid or unpaid, learn as much as you can!

Interrogation

An interview is not an interrogation, though it may feel like it. Stay focused and unflappable as you educate the audience on your value.

Interrupt

Do not interrupt when others are speaking, especially at a job interview. You'll be remembered for the wrong thing.

Interruptions

Interruptions happen at the strangest of times, some necessary, some not. Maintain your composure during interruptions at an interview.

Interview

An interview is a business conversation with a purpose—you are there to learn about them and they are there to learn about you, as equals!

Intuition

Pay attention to your intuition, the little voice that's ever-present, the voice that says "I'm here, listen. Don't ignore me."

Intuitive

When things don't feel right, seem right, or sound right, further investigate matters to find out why. Tap into your intuitive side!

Invent

Suppose you had to invent a job in order to earn a living. What work could you invent to generate revenue for yourself? *#ingenious*

Invest

A smart career move in today's competitive market is to invest in yourself—hire a career expert to guide you through the transition maze.

Investigation

Conduct a thorough investigation of the organization where you'll be interviewing. You may be asked, "What do you know about us?"

Investment

How much of a time investment will you devote weekly to your job search: 40+ hours? 30–40? 20–30? 10–20? Fewer than ten? With what results?

J JibberJobber to Joy

JibberJobber

The site JibberJobber.com is a valuable career management tool for today's job seeker invented by entrepreneur Jason Alba. Sign up today!

Job

A job is a chance to share your gifts, talents, and abilities with the world in exchange for a wage or salary that only you can agree to.

Job Description

If you don't have a job description, see if you can get one. Then target the text of your résumé to match the employer's specifications.

Job Hunter

A job hunter hunts and doesn't stop hunting until new employment is found. Move on to higher ground if at first you don't succeed.

JobHunter'sBible

This site of R.N. Bolles is a treasure trove of valuable info for today's job seeker: http://www.jobhuntersbible.com.

Jobless

Explain in a straightforward manner your reason for being jobless. Avoid a long, protracted explanation; keep it short and to the point.

Joblessness

Offer your reason for being between jobs at the beginning of the interview, not in the middle or end; you have nothing to hide!

Job Market

The job market is what the job market is. Whether it's good or bad, you still need a job! Don't let the market control you! You control you!

Job Offer

The time to negotiate any aspect of a job offer is after the offer has been extended to you and before you sign it! *#negotiate #everything*

Job Satisfaction

Job satisfaction is the by-product of a good job that's a good fit with you and who you are.

Job Search

Job search is a commonplace activity in today's tumultuous, bottom-line driven economy. Be prepared to go hunting many times! *#change*

Job Target

When you submit your résumé for a specific job, insert the name of the position and the Job ID#. Target the job. *#brand #focus*

Journal

Journal your thoughts. Keep track of how you are doing, just like your former employer did. Track your performance to measure your progress.

Joy

Joy is a gift that comes with meeting a new person, working in the right job, or sharing your expertise with others. *#happiness*

Keep to Knowledge

Keep

Keep private matters private, be it about yourself or an employer.

Key Words

Peruse your résumé for key words to align with the job target. Remember, computers scan for key words, often before humans get involved.

Kind

What kind of employee are you?

Kindness

Kindness is the gift you offer to others without expecting anything in return.

Knowledge

Knowledge is a weapon that will distinguish you from your competition.

L | Language to Luck

Language

Your language and the way you use it teaches others a lot about you and who you are. Does your language match your brand?

Laser

Laser focus is what is required today to find a job in today's competitive market. Job seekers either have it or they don't. Do you?

Lasting

Lasting relationships are a by-product of listening, laughing, and learning together.

Laugh

Laugh when you least feel like it—that sole activity may change your perspective from dark to light. *#jobsearch #jobhunt*

Launch

Launch the next chapter of your career from a strong mental and physical foundation instead of a weak and broken pile of rubble.

Leads

Ask others: Who do you know that would be helpful for me to meet? Who'd be willing to share their ideas, wisdom, or knowledge?

Learn

Learn from your mistakes and remember the ones you've already made so you don't repeat them.

Learning

Learning is life-long—whether you're a job seeker at 22 and starting in or a seasoned worker of 72 and starting over—keep learning!

Leave

When you lose your job, leave it behind you. Take with you your knowledge, skills, abilities, and cherished memories; let go of the rest.

Legacy

What would you like for others to remember about you when you depart Earth? Name five things you'd love for others to fondly recall.

Legal

Seek legal counsel when you don't understand an employment-related document. It is much easier to get into something than to get out of it.

Lend

Lend a hand to uplift someone's spirits in the good and not-so-good times that come with job search.

Length

The length of a job search is elusive and unknown and remains an active, ongoing process until receipt of a solid offer of employment.

Lesson

You don't need to learn the same lesson twice, whether it's learned the hard way or the expensive way.

Let

Let others know what you want and what you need; the greater the specificity on your part, the likelier your chances of success.

Let Go

Let go of the past; it is done. What, if anything, do you need to let go of to live a fuller, richer, and happier life now and tomorrow?

Let It Be

"Let it be" helps you realize there's no going back to what was or what might have been; there's only moving on to what is, what can be.

Letter

Within 72 hours of losing your job, write AND NEVER SEND a let-it-rip letter to the person(s) who fired you. Get it out; don't stuff it in!

Letters

Tuck in the back of your mind that cover letters may/may not be read by the hiring manager; be aware of this when writing your résumé.

Leverage

Leverage your skills to add value to an organization. What in your background and experience can you leverage for a competitive advantage?

Liabilities

Like any product for sale in today's global market, you bring particular assets and certain liabilities. What are yours in each category?

Lies

Don't lie. Lies are a tag-along; they stay with you and haunt you. Tell the truth and your life will be less complicated.

Like

Make a list of ten things you really like about yourself. During your darkest moments, pull out this list and read them aloud.

Likeability

Likeability is a key ingredient to getting hired. If people know you, like you, and trust you, that's a win-win-win formula to get hired.

Limit

If you were forced to limit your résumé to 300 words maximum (about one page), what 300 words would you intentionally pick? *#branding*

Link

Log on and link in to get a leg up in the competitive job search jungle. If you think it's a waste of time, please rethink your position.

Linkages

Look for links and linkages in your network. Who do you know that knows someone who is just the person you need to know?

LinkedIn

Create a profile on LinkedIn to strongly support you and your brand: be clear, credible, concise, and compelling: http://www.linkedin.com.

Listen

Talk twenty percent of the time and listen eighty percent. People will remember you. And the more you listen, the more you'll learn!

Lists

Create a daily to-do list for your job search; stick to it and evaluate your progress. Make adjustments as necessary to maximize success!

Little Things

Little things count and can make or break your success in the job search. Little things matter in big ways to employers.

Long-Term

What long-term goals do you expect to achieve in the next five, seven, and ten years?

Look

Look inside your heart, your head, and your soul—do you like what you see? What, if anything, needs to change?

Looking

Don't say to someone that you're looking around to see what's out there. The entire world is out there; define what you want then go get it.

Loser

You are not a loser if your job goes away! Get another one or get creative and build a business for yourself!

Loss

With the loss of your job comes an opportunity to start over, to start again, and to be something new and different if you will allow it.

Love

The love you have for your work reveals itself in all that you say, all that you do, and all that you can become in the days and years ahead.

Loyalty

What are you loyal to and how do you convey your loyalty to a person, place, or thing? What is your definition of loyalty in today's world?

Luck

What good fortune have you known, simply by chance or by luck?

M | Magic to Multiple Revenue Streams

Magic

What magic tricks, if any, have you integrated into finding a new opportunity?

Make Peace

Make peace with yourself about losing your job. What's done is done; you can't go back; you can only go forward with a forgiving heart.

Manage

Manage your job search the same way you would manage any other project; gather your resources, plan, prioritize, execute, and evaluate.

Manners

Mind your manners regardless of the environment. People notice and will remember poor manners. Always say thank you! *#etiquette*

Mantra

When you start each new day, what's the first thing you tell yourself? Consider: Is it positive or negative? Do you need a script rewrite?

Market

While the market may be tough, competitive, and ever-changing, tell yourself that you, too, are all of these things and more.

Marketing Materials

Do your career marketing materials, both online and offline, represent the very best of you, your product and its value? *#personal branding*

Master

Master the art of building relationships instead of honing the habit of gathering business cards. One lasts longer than the other.

Match

Match your traits to the qualities needed and desired by the prospective employer to best support your candidacy for the job.

Matter

If it doesn't matter, don't worry about it. Pay attention to what matters and let the rest go.

Maximize

With each and every word you speak or write, stop and ask yourself: Is this helpful or harmful for my brand and for my target audience?

Meals

When you participate in an interview where food and beverage is involved, avoid spills and speaking with a mouth full of food.

Meaning

What gives meaning and significance to your life? If you haven't thought about it, think about it.

Measurable

How will you measure your job search success? What strategies have you put in place to gauge your progress?

Meditation

When you're looking for a job, be intentional about time to celebrate quiet. No noise, no hustle, no bustle during moments of meditation.

Memorable Message

Make your meetings memorable and your message credible.

Memorize

Do not memorize answers to interview questions; get comfortable with answering a wide variety of questions in the interview.

Memory

Keep a short memory of all that's gone wrong in your career and a long memory of all that's been right about it. You'll consume less energy.

Mentally Prepare

Mentally prepare yourself to look for work. It's your new full-time job. Perform at your highest levels of productivity and efficiency.

Mentor

A great mentor provides true support, solid encouragement and real constructive criticism, including the hard things you don't want to hear!

Message

When people hear your name, what do you think is the first thing that comes to mind? (Usually a word or two, not a complete sentence.)

Methods

Whatever strategy works for you to find a job, use that one. Just because something worked for your buddy, doesn't mean it'll work for you.

Mind

Make up your mind to do something and then do it!

Mission Statement

Know the mission statement of your most recent employer and the mission statement of the prospective one. You may be asked to recite both.

Mistakes

Life is a series of sweet successes and mind-bending mistakes. Learn from both and go on. Don't dwell on what's done! #move #forward

Model

The twenty-first-century employment model in an ever-changing, price-driven, global market: "Here today, gone tomorrow."

Modify

Make a mental note of what's going well and what isn't as your job search and interview progresses; modify for maximum results.

Momentum

Plan to do something each and every day, 24/7, to maintain momentum in your quest for new employment.

Monetary Worth

What monetary worth does your product command based upon today's market needs, trends, and demands?

Money

How much money do you expect in return for your professional services? Is this sum of money fair, reasonable, and competitive?

Monitor

Monitor and manage your feelings and emotions about your past job and present circumstance, as both elements factor into your future.

Moral

What moral standards have you integrated into your job search?

Motivation

Job search motivation is something you either have or you don't, and you will either get or you won't. It's up to you to decide.

Motivators

What have you determined to be your best motivators when looking for a new opportunity?

Move Forward

Move forward with a positive spirit, an abundance of energy and an open mind as you recover, rethink, and rebuild your future.

Multiple Revenue Streams

There are many ways to earn income; what avenues and ideas have you considered to generate revenues for yourself and/or your family?

N Name to Nurture

Name

Protect your name and your reputation—they're sacred! Scroll to the "R" section and read the entry on "Reputation Defender."

Name-Dropping

While it is "who you know" that helps, dropping a person's name doesn't always work to your advantage. Use discretion. *#sensibility*

Necessary

Define the necessary ingredients of a good job for you. What elements matter most? What variables are optional?

Needs

First, identify the employer's needs and expectations; then, target and sell your knowledge, skills, and abilities to support their needs.

Negative Traits

Would others describe you as a negative person? If you had to claim one negative trait about yourself, what would it be and why?

Negativity

Negativity can be detected without a word being said.

Negotiate

Negotiate everything! If you don't know how to negotiate, talk to someone who does. Do not cheat yourself out of money that could be yours.

Negotiation

Negotiation puts more, not less, in your pocket! Be not afraid of this activity. If you can't negotiate for yourself, do it for your family!

Network

Your network can be large or small. In either case, it's up to you to build and sustain it to compete in today's ever-changing market.

Networking

Networking takes courage and stepping out of your comfort zone to meet new people. You may not like it; you just need to do it!

Net Worth

When you subtract your liabilities from your assets, what remains? What is your net worth to an organization? To yourself? To the world?

Never Give Up

If you give up now, you'll give up later on something that matters more.

New

Imagination creates new beginnings, new jobs, new ideas, new innovations, and new opportunities. What "new" do you imagine for yourself?

Next Step

Discover your next steps in the interview process prior to exiting the premises. As the conversation winds down, clarify and close.

Nice

In what ways do you demonstrate to a hiring manager that you are genuinely a nice person?

Niche

Do you fit in or stand out? Have you carved out a niche for yourself? If not, what do you need to do to make that happen?

No

"No" is the two-letter word you will hear time and again before you get to the three-letter word called "yes."

Non-Compete

Before you sign a contract for new employment, inquire about a non-compete so there are no surprises your first day on the job.

Nonsense

Consider the reliability and validity of information you're being told; does it make sense or is it pure nonsense?

Normal

This day, today, is the new normal. Don't live life waiting for yesterday's normal to return; that may never be. Work with today!

Note to Self

Cover letters may or may not be read. Whatever it is you want the employer to know, make certain it is stated in your résumé.
#note to self

Number-One-Position Mentality

You either have it or you don't, and it only takes seconds for others to determine if you're projecting a winning or a losing mentality.

Nurture

Nurture your network; you will reap abundant rewards by doing so. Keep in touch on a routine basis, not just in times of crisis.

O Objections to Outshine

Objections

Learn to overcome objections about your candidacy for the job. Speak about your assets and strengths, not your shortcomings. *#focus*

Observation

Sometimes, no words need to be said because all you need to know can be gained through observation. What will HR observe about Brand You?

Obstacles

Obstacles are part of job search. Don't let them stand in the way of getting to the opportunities. Remove 'em or move 'em!

Off Day

When you are having an "off day," do not make a big deal of it. Focus on making tomorrow a better one.

Offer

No matter what the offer, review it carefully to make certain that it aligns with your career needs, wants, and criteria for continued success.

One

What one job would you like to land? Remember, you're not looking for ten jobs, just one. What are you doing to find it?

O*NET

When you need to research various jobs in the U.S., this is a one-of-a-kind, free and powerful resource: http://online.onetcenter.org/.

Online

Online or offline, we still need each other to survive and thrive in today's competitive market place.

Online Presence

What, if anything, will people discover about you when they perform a Google, Bing, or other online search? Are you absent or present online?

Open

Keep your mind, head, and heart open to all possibilities and to learning, growing, and changing, regardless of age or circumstance.

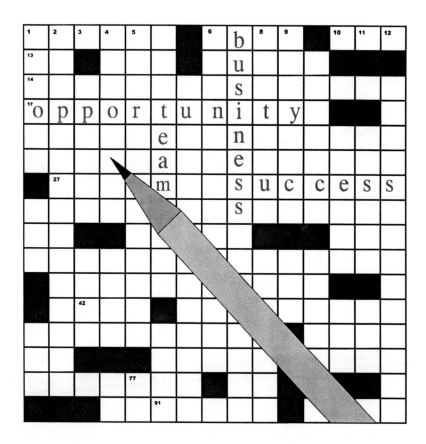

Opportunity

Opportunity is in front of you, behind you, on all sides of you; opportunity surrounds you if you open your eyes to it.

Optimism

Optimism is intentionally choosing a hopeful outlook over a hopeless one regardless of what is or isn't happening in the economy. *#mindset*

Optimize

Optimize your chances of getting noticed by the employer through your career-marketing documents online, offline, and in person.

Ordinary

Will a prospective employer consider you ordinary or extraordinary? What, if anything, can you do to become memorable and not *#forgettable*?

Organization

Organization is key to a successful job search campaign. If you're not organized, the competition will be, and you'll hurt your chances.

Others

You cannot rely on others to find you a job. You find the job with and through the support of others. *#persistent #attitude #relentless*

Outcome

What outcomes do you expect of yourself? If you have no specific expectations of self, what one(s) might you consider?

Outplacement

Outplacement is a career learning opportunity that employers provide, at their expense, to terminated employees. If offered, accept it!

Outshine

Name five ways you outshine your competition. What can you bring to the table that your competition can't?

Pack to Put

Pack

People love when you listen and care enough to remember the details. It says you're different than the rest of the pack. *#distinguish*

Packaging

Packaging is one component of the personal branding process. How have you chosen to package the product you?

Pages

Keep your résumé to one or two pages in most cases. Hiring managers don't have time to distill three to four pages of text. Think relevance!

Paradigm

The lens through which you see the world is your paradigm, yours and yours alone. What's your view?

Partnership

What do you bring to the table? What can you do for a business that it can't do without? Is it better off with you or without you?

Passions

What are your passions? What do you love to do? If you don't know, invite others to share their ideas at a Career Passion Party!

Patience

Patience is what it takes to discover a new opportunity in today's workplace. How much patience do you have? (You'll need a truckload!)

Pause

Pause to evaluate what you're doing in your job hunt; are you repeating the same thing over and over, but expecting different results?

Pay

Fill in the blanks: I want to make $__ I need to make $__. My bottom-line price range is: $__ to $__. And my walk-away price point: $__.

Pen

Take the appropriate tools to the interview: a smile, good pen, portfolio, notepad, business cards, résumés, and professional references.

Penmanship

If you write in cursive, make it legible. If you print, make it legible. Your penmanship is an extension of you and your brand.

People

It takes a team of people to help you find a job today. Have you built a talented team to help you find your next opportunity?

Performance

If you expect peak performance from self, you may achieve it. Conversely, if you expect little, don't be surprised when you get it.

Permission Slip

Pledge to self: With this permission slip, I now proclaim to me, myself, and I that I can and I will: _____.

Perseverance

Perseverance means you don't quit and you won't quit until you achieve your desired goal.

Persistence

Persistence is what separates you from your competition. Do not stop until you get what you want and need.

Personable

Are you personable? Is it easy for others to connect with you? When looking for work, this is a desirable quality to possess.

Personal Brand

Your individual (personal) brand embodies: what you stand for, why you stand out, and how you will add value in the eye of the beholder.

Personality

What unique and distinct traits do you possess that make you *you*? What parts of your personality do you like best? Least?

Perspective

What is your outlook? What is your perspective toward your job search and the future? Is it one of 1) pessimism, 2) optimism, or 3) realism?

Physical Fitness

Physical fitness communicates to the employer that you're invested in your own good health and well-being.

Plan

Remember when your grandmother told you to always have a Plan A, B, and C? She was right; you never know which one will work.

Planning

Planning is a good first step for job search success. Plan to find a job. Plan to succeed. Define, execute, evaluate as you move forward.

Plant

Plant the seeds of friendship. Tend with care over time and enjoy the harvest of your labor.

Politeness

Politeness is a quality that some have, some don't. Consider its importance and how it may be the one deciding factor in the hiring process.

Ponder

Something to ponder: Are you a job seeker or a potential business partner who delivers sound solutions to an organization's challenges?

Position

How you position your product is exactly how your audience will think about it. *#personal branding #competition #distinction*

Positive

In general, are you a positive, upbeat person? Do you look for the good side of things? Do you keep moving forward regardless? *#resilience*

Posting Online

When posting online, follow directions set forth by each specific organization. The process can vary from site to site. *#compliance*

Posture

Stand straight. Stand tall. Chin up! Head high! Look at yourself in the mirror. How would you describe your posture and overall carriage?

Power

Power up and power through the tough times until you find the right opportunity—full throttle ahead until you get what you want and/or need.

Practice

Practice is often the difference between you and the next candidate. Did you rehearse your lines at least 25 times? (Your competition will.)

Praise

Praise the talents of others to build professional friendships based on mutual respect and support of one another.

Predatory

Sadly, there are some people in business who will target you and prey upon you just because you're unemployed. Just say "no thanks!"

Preparation

Preparation is what you do before, not after, the implementation and execution of job search activities.

Prepare

Preparation is often the difference between winning and losing. It takes energy, commitment, and discipline to achieve desired results.

Prepared

Be absurdly and ridiculously overly prepared.

Presentation

Prepare for an interview by creating ten to twelve PowerPoint slides about Brand You, making the slides relevant to the job target.

Preserve

Preserve confidentiality of your relationships, conversations, and proprietary information. In short, keep the private stuff private.

Price

Know the price of product you. Do market research; negotiate compensation and benefits. Ask: what is a legitimate price range for my brand?

Pride

Put pride and ego aside; neither will generate revenues. Do not worry about what others will think as it only wastes precious energy.

Private Eye

Don't stay stumped; job search is a mystery to be solved. Are you a good private eye? If not, become one!

Probationary Period

Before accepting a job offer, ask about a probationary period, its duration as well as the employer's performance expectations.

Problem

What is your biggest career problem? What, if anything, can you do to fix it? Why do you have this problem in the first place?

Product

You're a product on sale in a very competitive market. Know your best work-related features, functions, and benefits before product launch.

Professionalism

Present yourself as a true professional through your words, actions, and deeds. How would you best describe your level of professionalism?

Profile

When you develop a profile for your résumé, make sure it embodies these three essential Es: experience, education, and employee traits.

Progress

How will you evaluate your job search progress? How will you know if you're progressing toward your goals? Define progress for best results.

Project

Respect your career management project as much as you respected any other project that you completed for an employer or for an instructor.

Project Management

As project manager of your career, you get to plan, organize, manage, execute, and evaluate each phase. How are you doing so far?

Promote

When you are looking for a job, promote Brand You, both online and offline, to maximize your chances of getting noticed by employers.

Promotion

Appropriate self-promotion is a necessity in today's competitive market. Apply both online and offline best practices for optimum results.

Pronounce

Pronounce words correctly and do not use "big words" if you don't know their meaning. You may be asked for a definition in an interview.

Pronouns

Before you send your résumé to a prospective employer, remove personal pronouns (I, me, my).

Pronunciation

Learn the correct pronunciation of a person's name prior to an interview—an important detail! Some people are super sensitive about this.

Properties

If you have a professional résumé writer create your résumé, be sure your name (not his or hers) appears in the Word document's Properties.

Proposals

You will go on several interview "dates" before someone offers you an employment proposal. That's how job hunting works today!

Protect

Protect your identity and your information both online and offline. Do not give out personal information or passwords! Protect yourself!

Purpose

Once you figure out what you were put here to do, go and do it. If you don't know what that is, that then becomes your purpose.

Purposefully

Purposefully, intentionally, and thoughtfully do something each and every day toward finding a new opportunity. Do not give up.

Purveyor

Your job is to become a professional purveyor of information about the wonderful product—you—and the value you bring to the table.

Put

Put on your thinking cap as you embark upon the job search journey. Think *unlike* everyone else is thinking to generate desired results.

Q Qualifications to Quit

Qualifications

What qualifications and credentials do you possess that align with your target job? Define them before writing a résumé or interviewing.

Qualities

What are your five best qualities that support your candidacy for your ideal job? Are they memorable or forgettable traits?

Quality

The quality of your job search demonstrates to the employer, in part, the quality of individual they would be acquiring and hiring.

Quantify

Quantify information in your résumé by using dollar amounts, numbers, and percentages to paint a visual image in the reader's mind.

Questions

When you go to an interview, remember to ask good questions—more than one and fewer than ten. Are you asking the right questions?

Quiet

Take time to be quiet with yourself. Clear your head, be still, don't think. Empty space to allow room for new ideas and inspirations.

Quietly

Quietly go out of your way to be there, especially when you know someone who is struggling and needs a comforting hand.

Quit

Don't quit looking for work until you find some. That's your job now! You don't have to like it, you just need to do it—and do it well!

R Reach to Rumors

Reach

Reach out to others when you are trying to find a new job. Ask for help. Do not say no for someone. Let them tell you they're too busy.

Ready

Are you ready to conduct an effective job search campaign or would you be better served by spending more time getting ready?

Realism

Today's job seeker gets to choose among pessimism, optimism, and realism. Which one best represents you and your brand?

Realistic

Just because you did a job in the past doesn't mean you'll do it again in the future. Things change; so can you! *#be #realistic #open #mind*

Reality

Face the fact that things are as they are, not as you may want them to be. What is the reality of your professional life right now?

Reason

If a prospective employer should ask, "Give me two good reasons *not* to hire you," what will be your response?

Reason for Leaving

On an employment application, cite the reason for leaving a job in truthful terms: downsized, job elimination, restructuring, acquisition.

Reciprocity

What do you offer employers in exchange for a paycheck? *#reciprocity*

Recognition

When you craft your résumé, remember to include professional recognitions, awards, honors, achievements, and results! Your competition will!

Recognize

Recognize that job search is the hardest job you'll ever have; keep telling yourself that you can and will do it, no matter what!

Recommendations

Invite four to six people to serve as professional recommendations. Advise them of your target goals and keep them apprised of progress.

Record Keeping

Record keeping is vital before, during, and after a job search. Keep track of everything in an offline or online system that works for you.

Recover

Give yourself time to grieve and recover from a job loss. To do otherwise is of detriment to your overall mental health and well-being.

Recruiter

View a recruiter as one of many valuable resources to support you in your quest for a new job. Listen, ask questions, learn, and be nice!

References

Know what your professional references will say about you. Also, what might they mention as areas for improvement?

Referrals

Referrals can be gleaned by asking your network for their recommendations to key decision makers in your target list of employers.

Regrets

What, if any, regrets do you have regarding your professional life? (Do not let your answer "do you in" at a job interview.)

Reinvent

You don't have to be what you were; you weren't born with a job title. Give yourself permission to try something new and reinvent yourself!

Reinvention

When considering job options, can you apply your existing skill set in a new and different way to generate revenue?

Rejection

Rejection comes in the form of a word called "no." Let it not stop you, stymie you, or stall you. Your competition won't allow it.

Relationships

The relationships you develop, cultivate, and sustain may pay big dividends in the future. Nurture your network on a consistent basis.

Relax

Relax and help the hiring team see you as a competent professional who is calm, focused, well rounded, and a pleasure to be around.

Relevant

What knowledge, skills, and abilities do you possess relevant to the job you seek? Decide now so you don't have to think about it later.

Relocation

Is relocation an option for you at this time in your career? Yes? No? Why or why not? You will be asked this question numerous times.

Remember

How do you want the employer to remember you? Decide beforehand and do not stray from your intended remembrance during the interview.

Remind

Remind yourself: have skills, will travel. It will help you realize that you can move on, that you can start over, and that you have much to offer.

Repel

Is there anything in your qualifications, credentials, or skill set that may repel the hiring manager? Consider this before your interview.

Replace

When considering job options, can you replace the job you had with a similar type of job or work activity to generate revenue?

Represent

Represent yourself with professionalism, confidence, enthusiasm, passion, and an unwavering sense of purpose until you find your next job.

Representative

You are your own best representative. Who better knows you than you? Make it easy and enjoyable for others to get to know you.

Reputation Defender

If you discover online digital dirt about yourself, contact http://www.reputationdefender.com to discuss their services and value to you.

Requirements

Scrutinize and analyze qualifications desired in a job posting. Engineer your résumé and cover letter to match the employer's requirements.

Research

Research pays. Learn about an organization's people, products, services, trends, changes, innovations, and competition before the interview.

Resilience

How would you best describe your resilience (bounce-back) quotient? Poor? Average? Excellent?

Resourceful

The more resourceful you are, the easier it will be for you to find or create a job for yourself.

Resources

Assemble the right mix of resources, from financial, physical, emotional, and spiritual to people, data, and things to help you succeed.

Respect

Respect yourself and then you can respect others.

Responsible

In the end and in the beginning, you are responsible for you. No one else has this right or this privilege. Take charge; take action—now!

Responsive

How responsive are you to the needs and requests of others? Do you get back to others without delay or are you too busy?

Rest

Rest is a gift you give yourself when you're looking for work. Looking for a job is exhilarating and exhausting. Rest up for the race!

Results

What results do you expect of yourself? What are the results others can expect of you? Is your résumé results driven? Think: #*competition*.

Résumé

Résumé defined: your Representative in your absence; Expression of excellence; Success driven; Unique; Meaningful; Extension of your brand.

Résumé Writer

There are millions of résumé writers, online and offline. Before you hire one, ask three to five people whom they recommend. Caveat emptor!

Retire

Which R of career transition is for you: Reinvent yourself, Replace with the same type of job, Retrain for a new job, or Retire?

Retirement

When considering job options, is retirement the best choice for you at this time in your life?

Retrain

When considering job options, is now the right time to pursue a degree, certification, designation, or other advanced education?

Retraining

When considering a retraining program, do extensive investigation into the program offering, costs, and potential for future employment.

Return on Investment (ROI)

If an organization buys you and your product, what ROI will they likely derive from the acquisition of Brand You?

Revenue

You can do one (or more) of three things for a company: cost it money, make it money (revenue), or save it money. Which will you do?

Rewards

What rewards do you expect from a career? What rewards might an organization derive through your affiliation with them?

Right

Always do the right thing in pursuit of new employment opportunities. Don't look back later and wish that you had done differently.

Ripoff Report

Before hiring a career-related firm, online or offline, first check to see if the business is listed at http://www.ripoffreport.com.

Road

You're the one who gets to choose the next road to travel. Steer carefully and stay on track until you arrive at your intended destination.

Roadblocks

There will be countless roadblocks in your job search path. Remain undeterred as you move over, under, around, and through them.

Role

Act the part, look the part, and play your role exceedingly well when you present yourself to the competitive work world.

Role Model

Who do you look up to? Who do you consider a role model? Who do you admire and respect? If possible, speak with them. Learn from the best!

Role-Play

Before you go to an interview, role-play your interview presentation at least 25 times to deliver a superb performance at the real deal.

Role-Playing

Role-playing for interview excellence can be done alone, standing in front of a mirror and critiquing yourself as you recite your lines.

Routine

Do create a routine and stick with it on a daily basis. Don't sleep in, watch television, or park yourself on the computer 24/7. *#jobhunt*

Rude

Expect that some people will be rude to you during the job search process. Do not let their shortcomings sway your mission and focus.

Rules

It will behoove you to learn job search rules of the twenty-first century as fast as you can. Ask, listen, learn and execute—play to win!

Rumors

Make your career decisions based on facts and knowledge, not rumor, innuendo, and speculation.

S | Salary to Surround

Salary

You're in charge of accepting or declining the salary offered you. Don't blame the employer later for what you knowingly agreed to earlier.

Salary Calculators

Google and Bing the phrase salary calculators (or pay calculators). Investigate at least three sites to analyze/compare/set a salary range.

Sales

You are in sales! From the time you get up until the time your head hits the pillow, you are in sales. To think otherwise is naïve.

Security

Companies can no longer guarantee you a lifetime of employment. Job security in today's market is as long as the day is—no more, no less.

See

Allow yourself to see things in a new light or with a different perspective; you may stumble upon different solutions and opportunities.

Seek

Seek is a verb. It requires action, motion, and devotion until you find whatever it is you're looking for.

Self-Reliance

Rely upon your skill set to move you from project to project, be it as an employee, a contractor, or other partnership arrangement.

Sell

Sell what you have, not what you don't, with respect for the knowledge, skills, and abilities that you've been given to serve others.

Sense of Humor

A sense of humor can keep you moving forward when your burdens get too heavy and you're feeling totally overwhelmed.

Senses

Pay attention to your external senses (hearing, sight, taste, touch, smell) during an interview to get a good overview of the organization.

Share

Share your talents and share your knowledge, and you will make someone's life easier, better, or happier by doing so.

Shoes

Your shoes are part of your brand message; what do yours convey? Make sure they are clean and polished and, women, no spike heels.

Shortcut

If your shortcut doesn't work, then it really isn't a shortcut, is it?

Simple

Do not make job search more complicated than it needs to be. Remember—keep it simple and stupid! (#*Clarence "Kelly" Johnson*)

Skills

Make a list of your top five transferable skills (nouns or "ing" words) that you: 1) like, 2) do easily, and 3) want to do in the future.

Smile

A smile is an important distinguishing factor during the highly competitive interview process; use it to your advantage. #*personality*

Soar

At an interview, remember to S-O-A-R: address the Situation, Obstacle, Action step, and Result to easily answer behavioral-style questions.

Social Media

Optimize social media in your search. Blog, post good comments, and tweet. (If employed and looking, some employers ban these activities.)

Social Networking

Like it or not, social networking and social media play major roles in twenty-first-century job search activities. Are you in or out of the game?

Solo

While you may get to the end goal going solo, you'll improve your chances with a talented team invested in your career success!

Sound

How do you sound when you speak: confident, afraid, nervous, angry, positive, negative? Listen to yourself; what will others hear?

Speak

Speak well of others every chance you get and it will reflect positively on you and your brand.

Specifications

Analyze the organization's job specifications to determine if the job is a good fit with you, your knowledge, skills, and interests.

Specify

Be specific, not vague, about the type of work you desire so others can help you get what you want. *#specify*

Spirituality

What role, if any, does spirituality play in your world as you explore new career opportunities?

Standards

Conduct yourself with the highest standards of professionalism and excellence each and every day of your life. *#personal #brand #remarkable*

Stand Out

Stand out in a good and appropriate way! Among five first-rate candidates, what makes you the one the hiring team should pick?

Stand Up

Stand up for yourself. If you don't, who will?

Start

Ask yourself: what do I need to start doing and what do I need to stop doing to achieve my job search goals?

Stay Focused

Stay focused. You can paint the house after you get a job. You can clean the closet after you find work. Do not get sidetracked! *#prioritize*

Step Up

Step up and do what you need to do, no matter how hard, difficult, uncomfortable, or challenging it is; you will be a better person for it.

Steward

Be a good steward of the many gifts and talents that have been bestowed upon you. Use them wisely and well to serve others.

Stop

Stop doing what doesn't work when looking for a job and start doing what does! Devise a new system—one that works for you, not against you.

Stop-Thinking Strategy

If you find yourself thinking in negative ways, hit the shut-off valve and stop thinking that way. Switch to a strategy of positive thought!

Story

Your work life is a story and you are the one who gets to tell it. How does your story go?

Stranger

Avoid being the stranger to a prospective employer; get known, get recommended, get hired!

Strategy

Strategy is one of the single best things that you can develop to get from here to there. Innovate, execute, and evaluate to win the offer.

Strengths

Know with certainty and clarity your best strengths. Apply them fully and with excellence to well serve others.

Stress

There are two kinds of stress: distress and eustress. One may prevent you from achieving your goals; the other can propel you forward.

Stressors

Make a list of what's stressing you and see what, if anything, you can do to alleviate stressors or, at the very least, manage them.

Strive

Strive to do your best in all ways and always.

Stuck

Being stuck is a sad, bad, and unhappy place that can lead to a better spot if you are willing to try and get out of your rut.

Succeed

What do you need to succeed? This is a basic and fundamental question that is good to ask yourself (and others) on a routine basis.

Success

Define what "success" means to you, and then you will know when you are a success based upon your own definition!

Sucks

Make a list of what sucks, in your opinion, about your job search. What, if anything, can you do about it?

Supervisor

What will your most recent supervisor say about you and your work? What will your former supervisors say about your performance?

Support

Build a team of people who support you and care about you without condition, without restriction, and without monetary gain. *#supportive*

Surround

Surround yourself with people who build you up instead of bring you down! Life is hard enough; who are your true fans and who must you drop?

T Talent to Two

Talent

Make it easy for the person who's interviewing you to learn of your talent. Do not make them drag information out of you.

Talk

Always listen more than you talk. You'll almost always learn something and it could be the one thing that changes the course of your life.

Talking

Excessive talking will not give you an edge but an exit! Do not give your interviewer a reason to prematurely end the conversation.

Target

Develop a list of first, second, and third tier employers of interest. Research internal and external contacts who'll help and support you.

Task

Looking for a job in today's competitive market is a task requiring tenacity, unwavering commitment, and relentless pursuit of the goal.

Tax Deductions

Keep track of all monies invested in your job search. Discover what can and can't be deducted in accordance with IRS regulations.

Teach

Teach your listener exactly what it is you offer and how it will add value and benefit to the organization.

Team

Job search is best done as a team sport, not an individual activity. Increase your chances of success with a team-driven approach.

Technical

Lacking technical competency? Investigate learning opportunities in your local area or online to enhance your skill set.

Techniques

Integrate multiple job search techniques to uncover career opportunities; do not rely on a single strategy to produce the desired results.

Technology

Technology is a tool that affords job search ease and efficiency. It is not a substitute for building relationships; people hire people.

Teeth

Before you go to employment interviews, clean and whiten your teeth. Your smile telegraphs much about you and your brand.

Tell

Tell somebody that you love, or at least like, when you're downsized, terminated, fired, made redundant, or dooced. Reach out for support!

Temporary

Consider temporary job assignments or interim consulting projects while you're looking for new employment opportunities.

Tenacity

T-e-n-a-c-i-t-y = Temperament, endurance, needs, attitude, commitment, investment, time, you!

Termination

Ask about employer-sponsored outplacement or career transition services when you lose your job. If offered such services, participate.

Tested

Pay attention in an interview. If you're interrupted, be sure to keep track of the last thing said; your attention span may be tested!

Testimonial

A well-written testimonial presents who, what, when, where, why, and how of you, your brand, and its value. Think: LinkedIn recommendations.

Thank You

Consistently express your thanks and appreciation via voice messages, handwritten notes, emails, texts, or tweets. Employers notice!

Think

Think positively every day. Make a list of twenty positive traits and ten negative traits about yourself. Focus on the positives daily!

Think Differently

If things are not going your way in your job search, what, if anything, can you do to change your thinking and do something differently?

Thinking

Don't waste too much time thinking on the employer's dime. Prepare well in advance and be efficient in your presentation. *#interviewing*

Think Tweet

When writing your résumé or interviewing, be succinct, relevant, excellent, appropriate. Think: Twitter. Think: tweet!

Third

The upper one-third of page 1 of your résumé provides proof of three things: 1) who you are, 2) what you want, 3) why you can do the job!

Third Party

A third party speaking on your behalf adds credibility to your brand. Align the testimonial in your résumé with your target job.

Time

Clarify before an interview the exact appointment time and the time allocated for the interview. Arrive no more than ten minutes early.

Title

You weren't born with a job title branded to your forehead. Don't let the job title that *was* define now what *is*. *#change #transition*

Tone of Voice

Your voice tone conveys much about you. What message are you projecting to your target audience? Happy, sad, up, down?

Toolbox

Pack your career transition "toolbox" with the essential knowledge, skills, and abilities you will need to execute a successful job search.

Tools

What are the tools you need to succeed as a focused, successful job seeker? Assemble them now to support your #*success*.

Tough

In a tough job market, decide that you'll be tougher in getting what you want and need to make your life work.

Track

Track your performance as you explore new opportunities. What's working? What's not? What, if anything, can you change for better results?

Track Record

A track record is your footprint of the past. It's about where you've been and it stays with you forever. What's your track record to date?

Trade

Trade school may be an option for you if you're not interested in pursuing a two- or four-year college degree. Explore possibilities.

Train

Train and educate your target audience about the product you and the best features, benefits, and value of your brand.

Transferable

Transferable skills are the competencies and abilities you offer an employer in exchange for a paycheck. What are yours?

Transition

Transition is a process whereby one acknowledges change and works daily to move from Point A to Point B in a purposeful, intentional way.

Transition Suitcase

When you go on a trip, you pack a suitcase. Think transition trip: load your suitcase with skills you'll need for a successful journey!

Travel

If air travel is required to go to an interview, the prospective employer may/may not pay for it—use good judgment before you book a flight.

Treatment

Treat others the way you want them to treat you. What you give to the world is what you get back. *#brand*

Trends

Stay current with recent trends, changes, and marketplace happenings to sustain a competitive advantage as you explore new opportunities.

Trial

A trial period of employment is a chance where you get to prove to the employer that you were the right hire and not the wrong one.

Trials

Trials and tribulations go hand-in-hand with any job or career in today's volatile, ever-changing market place.

Trick

As a job seeker, the trick is to figure out what you're good at and then to find someone who will give you a chance to prove it!

Triumph

Triumph over the obstacles, setbacks, detours, and distractions that will confront you as you move forward in your career journey.

Trust

Trust your heart and head to make the best career decisions possible based on thorough due diligence. Making no decision is a decision.

Trustworthy

If you say that you are trustworthy, people may doubt you, but if you show proof through example, people may very well believe you.

Truth

Share truthful information on résumés and at interviews. Avoid too many details; answer what's been asked and stop talking. Period.

Try

Try is a word that can produce life-changing results. What do you need to try?

Turnoff

What, if anything, are the habits that you employ that could be turnoffs to an employer? What, if anything, can you do to alleviate them?

Twitter

Twitter your way to a new job. Go here: http://twitter.com and browse here: www.twitterjobsearch.com/.

Two

Time and talent are two Ts to clarify at an interview's start: How much time do we have together today? Can you describe the ideal talent you seek?

U Undergird to Until

Undergird

Undergird your career with competence, caring, and character. You will stand out in a sea of competition.

Unemployed

Instead of telling someone you're *unemployed*, say *in transition* or *between jobs*, better accepted phrases than words like *fired* or *jobless*.

Unexpected

The one thing you can count on with certainty in a job search is the unexpected; anticipate the best and prepare for the worst.

Unfriend

If one of your social network connections is in any way blemishing your brand, unfollow or unfriend them. Protect thy brand name!

Unique

If you don't know what makes you unique and distinct, you're not ready to look for a job. What distinguishes you from your competitors?

Unstuck

Only you can decide to get unstuck. You can stay mired where you are or you can start digging your way out, one spoonful at a time.

Until

Do not give up on the career search until you get what you want, or need, to make your life work.

V Vacancy to Vulnerability

Vacancy

At the interview, ask the hiring manager why the position is vacant; you may discover an important, telling piece of information. Listen!

Vacation

While you may be interested in vacation and benefits, do not inquire about such until a mutual interest has been established. *#important*

Vague

Vague and ambiguous will not support your candidacy for a job. Cite specific examples to align your credentials with an employer's needs.

Value

Know your value. Do not launch your job search until you can speak with clarity, confidence, and conviction about your value and worth.

Value Proposition

What are you offering and what is the perceived value to the prospective employer in buying Brand You? *#personal branding #competition*

Values

What are the values that make you the person you are? Make a list in case the hiring manager asks. *#do #not #compromise #values*

Variables

Consider all of the variables of a job opportunity before accepting an employer's offer. There are other factors to consider beyond money.

Verbal

On a scale of one (poor) to ten (outstanding), how do you rate your verbal skills? What, if anything, can you do to enhance them?

Verbs

Inject energy and interest in your résumé through careful insertion of the best verbs to convey the best story about the amazing Brand You!

Victory

What is the biggest victory you've known in your career to date? What do you have planned for your next one?

Visibility

Visibility, online and offline, is a requisite for today's job search. If you can't be found, you're hurting your chances of getting hired.

Vision

What is your vision for you in the next 30, 60, and 90 days? In the next one, three, five years? Know this before you go to an interview.

Visual

What is one easy, simple thing you can do to improve your overall visual image? Will you do it? Why or why not?

Voice

How does your voice sound and what, if anything, have others told you about your voice?

Voice Message

Create a voice message that sounds appropriate, energetic, and professional, be it on your landline or mobile phone.

Voices of Others

The voices of others lend credibility to what you're saying about yourself. Identify those in your circle who'll speak well on your behalf.

Volunteer

Willingly and freely volunteer your time and talent to enrich others' lives. The by-product is that your own life will be richer for it!

Vulnerability

Your vulnerability may be preyed upon when you are at your lowest point, weakest moment, or greatest time of need. *#heads up*

Want to Wimpy Handshake to Wow Factor

Want

What do you want and what will it take to get it? What are you willing to give up? What are you willing to sacrifice to get what you want?

Want Ads

The want ads are one resource for job leads; add other resources to your search, using both online and offline sources in your job hunt.

Waste

Waste no time in offering support, guidance, and encouragement to help others who are also looking for a job. Share and learn together.

Weakness

What is your biggest weakness and what have you done to address it and/or alleviate it? You'll be asked about it in an interview.

What If

Stop asking so many "what if" questions and do something constructive to help yourself.

When

When you ask "why" sorts of questions, be careful; some people may get defensive. Consider using a counseling line: "Help me understand."

Where

Where do you want to live, work, and play? Pick your top three to five places and investigate opportunities in those specific areas.

Whiner

Are you a whiner? Yes? No? If you are, why are you and what are you getting out of it?

Who

Who are you? Make it easy for the hiring manager to learn about you through words you freely offer in educating them about Brand You.

Why

Instead of wondering "Why me?" in response to your job loss, consider another perspective: "Why not me?"

Will

The will to do whatever it takes—legally, morally, ethically—to get on down the road of life to the next opportunity, will you do it?

Wimpy Handshake

A wimpy handshake conveys a lack of confidence. Find someone to shake hands with, and then ask for their candid feedback. Practice pays!

Win

A job is yours to win and yours to lose in a competitive market. Are you thinking like a winner or a loser as you knock on doors?

Winner

If asked to grade yourself on a scale of one to ten (ten = tops), what's your score? (Don't pick ten; no one's perfect!) *#winner*

Word Choice

Be mindful of your word choice. One wrong word can cost you the job. Think first! You can't take back what's said in the interview!

Word of Mouth

Word of mouth remains one of the best, most powerful, and effective ways to find a job. Where are you spending your time? *#results*

Words

In an interview, choose words that sound positive; know that each word you share either supports or jeopardizes your candidacy for the job.

Work

Work at something that you like and enjoy more than something you hate and despise. You'll be happier and healthier.

Work Ethic

Develop and sustain an incredible work ethic. You will stand out.

Worry

Don't worry before you have to.

Worth

Know your worth to an organization and be able to articulate the value the employer will derive through the acquisition of Brand You.

Worthy

Can you cite five factors that make you a worthy contender for the job that you would love to do? *#competitive #advantage*

Wow Factor

Do you have a "wow factor?" How would you describe it? If you don't have one, what do you need to do to get one?

X-ray

X-ray

X-ray your career to evaluate what's gone well for you in the past and what you'd like to change in the future.

Y | Yes to Youth

Yes

Say yes to a job you want and no to one you don't. Otherwise, neither you nor the employer will be happy or satisfied with the mismatch.

Yesterday

In the yesterday of your life, what did others "want" you "to be" when you grew up? Others could be your family, teachers or friends.

You

No matter what name you call it: You Inc., Me Inc., CEO of You, or Brand You, your continued career success begins and ends with y-o-U!

Young

Young or not so young, you still need to find a job—unless you've won the lottery. Whether you're 22 or 72, go get your piece of the pie.

Youth

As a youth, what did you dream of doing for a job when you reached adulthood? Are you doing that now and, if not, why not?

Z Zany to Zip

Zany

What zany idea do you have for a business or a job? Who, if anyone, is already doing your idea? What, if anything, can you learn from them?

Zeal

Zeal is what it takes to find a new job in today's economy. Do you have it?

Zest

Let the employer see your zest, energy, and enthusiasm in your interview presentation. What you deliver decides your future.

Zip

Zip it when it comes to making negative remarks about persons, places, or past employers. Let the positives prevail!

Tweet Tips

(Please add your own tweet tips here. If there's a particular tweet you would like to share, send it along to Happy About at http://happyabout.com/ for possible inclusion in a second edition.)

Reminders/Things to Remember:

About the Author

Billie Sucher is a nationally-known career transition expert, outplacement consultant, professional résumé writer, speaker, author, poet, and prolific blogger for Career Hub, http://www.careerhubblog.com. For over two decades, she has provided professional career management services to organizations and individuals throughout the country (from entry level to executive level), doing so with an unwavering commitment to and passion for:

- Career Consulting, Counseling, and Coaching

- Professional and Executive Résumé Writing

- Company-sponsored Outplacement and Career Transition Programs (Group/Individual)

- Personal Branding for Competitive Advantage

- Interview Coaching to Win the Offer

- Public Speaking and Seminars on Career Topics

Sucher holds a Master's degree in Counseling from Drake University and numerous industry certifications including International Job and Career Transition Coach, Career Management Alliance Credentialed Career Manager Distinction, and William Bridge's Transition Management Certification. Her résumé and cover letter work is featured in twenty-eight national best-selling books. Earlier this year, Billie was named one of the *150+ Experts on Twitter ALL Job Seekers MUST Follow* and one of the *50 Personal Branding Consultants Worth Working With*. The author of 'Between Jobs: Recover, Rethink, Rebuild,' and 'Baseball for Life®' perpetual calendar, she invites you to visit her website, follow her on Twitter, or connect with her on LinkedIn:

http://www.billiesucher.com

http://www.careerhubblog.com

http://www.LinkedIn.com/in/billiesucher

http://twitter.com/billiesucher/

Other Happy About® Books

Purchase these books at Happy About http://happyabout.info or at other online and physical bookstores.

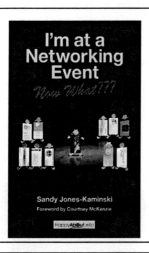

I'm at a Networking Event—Now What???

Through this book you will learn how to make quality connections, cultivate relationships, expand your circle of influence through networking events, and create good "social capital."

Paperback: $19.95
eBook: $14.95

Internet Your Way to a New Job

This book will provide you what you need to know and step you through the process of online job searching, professional branding, social and professional networking, and career building with uncomplicated advice, tips, and techniques on how to effectively find a new job and grow your career.

Paperback: $19.95
eBook: $14.95

Happy About My Resume

The average recruiter or hiring manager spends less than 15 seconds reviewing a resume. Most people's resumes fail to "wow" the reader and quickly end up in the "no" pile.

Paperback: $19.95
eBook: $14.95

The Successful Introvert

The purpose of this book is to present strategies used by successful people—including numerous celebrities—in managing their introversion or shyness while becoming successful in professional endeavors.

Paperback: $19.95
eBook: $14.95

LaVergne, TN USA
05 April 2010
178175LV00003B/1/P